# TEXTURE

## the essence of wood, linen, stone & wool

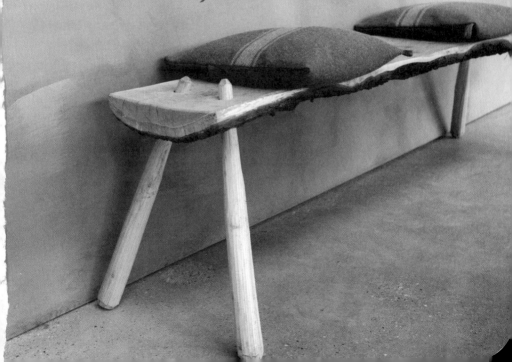

# TEXTURE

## the essence of wood, linen, stone & wool

RYLAND PETERS & SMALL
LONDON • NEW YORK

**Designer** Maria Lee-Warren
**Editor** Annabel Morgan
**Production Controller** Mai-Ling Collyer
**Art Director** Leslie Harrington
**Editorial Director** Julia Charles
**Publisher** Cindy Richards

**Text** Hilary Mandleberg

Originally published as four separate titles:
*Essence of Wood*, *Essence of Linen*, *Essence of
Stone* and *Essence of Wool*.

This combined edition published in 2015
by Ryland Peters & Small
20–21 Jockey's Fields
London WC1R 4BW
and
Ryland Peters & Small, Inc.
341 E 116th Street,
New York, NY 10029
www.rylandpeters.com

10 9 8 7 6 5 4 3 2 1

Text © Hilary Mandleberg and Ryland Peters
& Small 2015.
Design and commissioned photography
© Ryland Peters & Small 2015
See page 208 for full picture credits.

ISBN: 978 1 84975 668 6

A CIP record for this book is available from
the British Library.

Printed and bound in China

# CONTENTS

# INTRODUCTION

This book celebrates the textures of the natural world — wood, linen, stone and wool — and shows how they can enhance and enliven our homes. It aims to provide some decorating inspiration as well as a little information about the surfaces we choose to surround ourselves with.

Any interior designer will tell you that using contrasting textures in an interior is the key to a successful scheme. The human eye is designed to discern difference; it revels in variety and constantly seeks new interest. Texture adds depth, detail and definition. It draws us into a space and invites us to linger; to run our fingers over different surfaces, caress cashmere or stroke old wood. And it's most important in a room with a limited colour scheme.

Different textures evoke different moods. Rough, unfinished textures such as undyed linen and weathered wood feel warm and natural and signal rustic charm. Polished marble and ironed linen, on the other hand, are cool, sleek and formal. Pick and choose wisely for the desired effect. Throw a chunky woven rug over old floorboards or layer crumpled linen with a fluffy mohair blanket. Contrast heightens the effect – weathered wood will appear more rugged alongside gleaming granite, for example. As this book demonstrates, three or four distinct textures, carefully balanced, will make any space come to life.

# WOOD

WHEN WE USE THE TREE
RESPECTFULLY AND
ECONOMICALLY, WE
HAVE ONE OF THE
GREATEST RESOURCES
ON THE EARTH.

FRANK LLOYD WRIGHT

# FIRE AND SHELTER

Fire and shelter are two of life's essentials. Wood offers us both. It warms us and enables us to prepare food. And it protects us from wind and rain, sun and snow. For millions of years, wood has been a mainstay of human existence. It has provided us with one of the most beautiful, versatile and durable of our building materials and in many parts of the world it is still an important source of fuel.

For our ancestors, supplies of wood were readily available for building. It was a good insulator and protector from the elements. To build a wall, people could gouge notches in logs and stack them one on top of the other, log-cabin style. Or they could use slices of tree trunks to construct a framework, filling the gaps between with a mixture of thick mud and twigs. As building techniques developed and became more sophisticated, they learned to slice, shave and plane wood into boards or tiles. Laid centuries ago in overlapping patterns, these still keep homeowners warm and dry today.

OAK LOGS WILL WARM YOU WELL
THAT ARE OLD AND DRY
LOGS OF PINE WILL SWEETLY SMELL
BUT THE SPARKS WILL FLY.

TRADITIONAL ENGLISH FOLK SONG

# NEXT TO NATURE

In a rural setting, nothing beats wood that seems to have come straight from the forest. It breathes life and soul into a building, introduces warmth and texture and gives us a spiritual link with nature and with ancient human beliefs.

In ancient Norse mythology, Yggdrasil was an immense ash tree that held heaven in its branches, the underworld in its roots and all temporal life in its vast trunk. We can bring this sense of majesty and wonder into our own homes by introducing the elemental grandeur of rough-hewn logs or the twists and turns of bark-covered branches, complete with the cracks and fissures that tell of a tree's history.

BRING HOME THE BEAUTY OF NATURE. SHOWCASE THE NATURAL CURVES AND RHYTHMS OF WOOD AND CELEBRATE ALL ITS VARIOUS TEXTURES.

# CONTEMPORARY

As a building material, wood is tremendously versatile; it can be adapted to any number of locations and to all historical periods. One of the motifs of the last hundred years or so has been man's domination of nature, so it is no surprise to find that in the modern home, wood often reflects this theme. Nowadays, we cut, plane, sand and polish wood into smooth, sleek shapes that emphasize its grain and texture. We slice it into thin veneers and bend it into sinuous shapes. We combine it with slate, leather and steel. In short, we force it to obey our rules.

IN CONTEMPORARY INTERIORS, WOOD
SETS THE SCENE IN STYLE. VENEERED
CABINETS ARE SLEEK YET RICHLY
GRAINED. WOOD-CLAD WALLS BRING
WARMTH TO A MINIMALIST INTERIOR.
BROAD PLANKS OF SOLID ASH ARE WARM
YET FUNCTIONAL UNDERFOOT.

# CARVED AND DECORATED

Decorated and painted wood leads us into new realms, where woodcarvers, turners, artists and decorators reign supreme. The urge to embellish our homes is a deep-seated, primitive one and wood offers us myriad possibilities. Walls and staircases can be panelled and stencilled, bedsteads carved, stair rails turned to

form barley-sugar twists, floors laid in geometric blocks or precision-edged with the finest marquetry, roofs fretted into hearts and flowers and knick-knacks graced with light-as-air motifs.

I FREQUENTLY TRAMPED EIGHT OR TEN MILES THROUGH THE DEEPEST SNOW TO KEEP AN APPOINTMENT WITH A BEECH-TREE, OR A YELLOW BIRCH, OR AN OLD ACQUAINTANCE AMONG THE PINES.

HENRY DAVID THOREAU

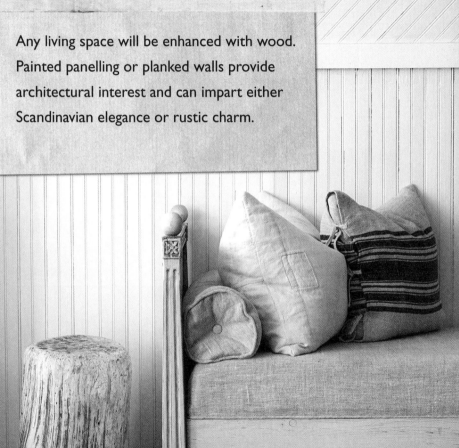

# LIVING SPACES

Any living space will be enhanced with wood. Painted panelling or planked walls provide architectural interest and can impart either Scandinavian elegance or rustic charm.

Wood's strength and weight vary greatly from species to species, so different woods suit different purposes. Softwoods come from coniferous evergreen trees and are easy to cut, while hardwoods come from deciduous trees, have a closer grain and take a high polish. Despite their names, hardwoods are not always harder than softwoods and vice versa. Their colours range widely, too, from the white wood of holly through the warm hues of giant redwoods to the black of ebony. Some woods have a natural lustre or – as in the case of cedar – a rich odour from the essential oils they contain. The most beautiful woods are often sealed and polished to show off their natural good looks, while others can be painted or stained to hide their humble origins.

WOOD CAN BE
EVERYWHERE IF YOU
CHOOSE. RICH POLISHED
WOOD TAKES A MODERN
KITCHEN TO NEW HEIGHTS.
A BROAD OAK TABLE AND
FINELY TURNED CHAIRS
MAKE A CEREMONY OF
DINING. EXPOSED BEAMS
AND A WOODEN FLOOR
CAN EVOKE A SPACIOUS
MEDIEVAL HALL.

Whether you long for a pile of cosy quilts or pared-down linen sheets, wood works brilliantly in the bedroom. What could be more appealing than a night spent beneath the eaves in a room striped with ancient oak beams? In a modern home, a headboard fashioned from salvaged planks adds warmth and texture to an interior.

# BEAUTY AND UTILITY

From simple hand-turned spoons to fine furniture, there are an estimated ten thousand different products made of wood, and of these home accessories are but a few. Wood brings us tactile platters and bowls that please the eye and finely turned candlesticks, cups, boxes and frames that feel smoothly sensuous to the hand. As a raw material, its countless possibilities inspire the maker. It needs only a little creativity to transform twigs and branches into rustic furniture that speaks of the woods, or to stamp scrolling foliate designs onto a sheet of delicate veneer to create an interior that hints at a fantastical forest.

# ALFRESCO

Nowhere is wood more at home than out of doors. Trees are our planet's lungs and as such are a major focus of environmental concerns. As long as we take care of them, they will repay us in kind by providing for our needs.

Wood outdoors is a must for anyone who loves nature. A wooden house rising tall in the midst of a forest or perched beside a lake is at one with its surroundings. Painted or plain, wooden porches and verandahs are where indoors and outdoors meet. Take a seat and watch the world go by from a bench or settle into deep cushions. Mark out your space with a picket fence or merge into the background at a long table. Use wood outdoors and feel yourself part of a long tradition.

**TO DWELLERS IN A WOOD, ALMOST EVERY SPECIES OF TREE HAS ITS VOICE AS WELL AS ITS FEATURE.**

'UNDER THE GREENWOOD TREE'
THOMAS HARDY

# LINEN

LOVE IS LIKE LINEN;
THE OFTEN CHANGED,
THE SWEETER.

JOHN FLETCHER

Dating back many thousands of years to ancient Mesopotamia, through the centuries linen has been worn by rich and poor alike. When synthetics took the hard work out of fabric care, it fell from favour but in recent years we have come to appreciate the aesthetic and practical advantages of this fabric.

Linen (or *Linum usitatissimum*, to give the fabric its botanical name) is made from fibres extracted from stems of flax, a plant that grows everywhere that the climate is temperate and moist and that requires few pesticides or fertilizers. In modern times, central Europe, as well as Ireland and the United States, have all enjoyed thriving linen industries that only started to decline when cheaper cotton came on the scene.

FINE LINEN WITH BROIDERED WORK FROM EGYPT WAS THAT WHICH THOU SPREADEST FORTH TO BE THY SAIL; BLUE AND PURPLE FROM THE ISLES OF ELISHAH WAS THAT WHICH COVERED THEE.

**EZEKIEL 27:7**

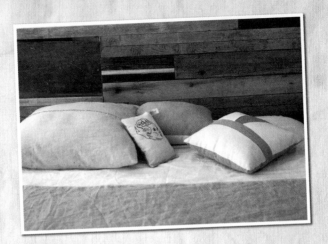

Linen manufacture has hardly changed since ancient times. Its long and laborious journey from flax field to cloth is marked by several different stages, including the soaking of the stems to loosen them from the stalk ('retting'), crushing and beating of the stalks ('scutching') and combing or 'hackling', to remove the shorter lengths from the long, soft flax fibres. After the fibres have been separated, they are spun into yarn or woven or knitted into linen textiles.

In ancient times, garments made of white linen were prized as symbols of purity and were used by the Egyptians and, later, the Jews, for religious ceremonies. Today, linen is for every day. Clothes and fabric designers adore the material; it is cool, absorbent and hardwearing. From fine sheers to heavy weaves, it suits all styles and seasons. The only fabric to improve on washing, crease-resistant treatments now make linen even better.

# SPINNING A YARN

Even after years of use, an old linen grain sack can still charm its way into a modern home, for part of linen's enduring appeal lies in its varied textures. After combing, the flax is spun. Wet spinning softens the gums in the fibres and produces fine, regular yarn used for clothing. Dry spinning gives the heavier yarn needed for canvas, furnishing fabrics, and many other household textiles. A handkerchief or shirt might be in a plain weave, while a firm, close, twill weave is used for curtains or suiting.

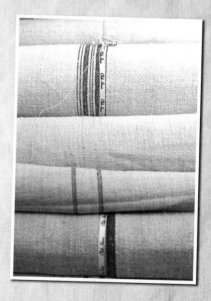

Our current love affair with all things natural means that unbleached linen's brownish hue and the creamy white of bleached linen have found new favour. But colour rules, too, and has done for centuries. Some linens found in Egyptian tombs were dyed using vegetable dyes such as indigo, madder and saffron. Today, we have a huge range of long-lasting synthetic dyes at our disposal, and linen just soaks them up thirstily.

**ECLECTIC STYLE**

linen cushions create
a cosy seating nook

antique linen sheets
make a dainty curtain

vintage linen reinvented
as cushion covers

different weaves and
weights provide contrast

Linen could be described as the Jekyll and Hyde of the textile world. This versatile fibre is just as much at home in the shape of fine woven fabrics and lace as it is in heavy-duty sacking and twine. Hence its ability to blend easily with a multitude of decorating styles, from relaxed rustic simplicity to pared-down urban chic and everything in between.

monogrammed vintage linen covers a sofa

linen dish cloths hung out to dry

A WHITE-PAINTED BEDROOM WITH THICK WALLS AND TILED FLOOR IS SAVED FROM BEING COLD AND UNINVITING THANKS TO A BED DRESSED IN THE SOFTEST VINTAGE LINEN. AND CUSHION COVERS MADE FROM ANTIQUE SACKS WILL SOFTEN ANY MODERN SOFA.

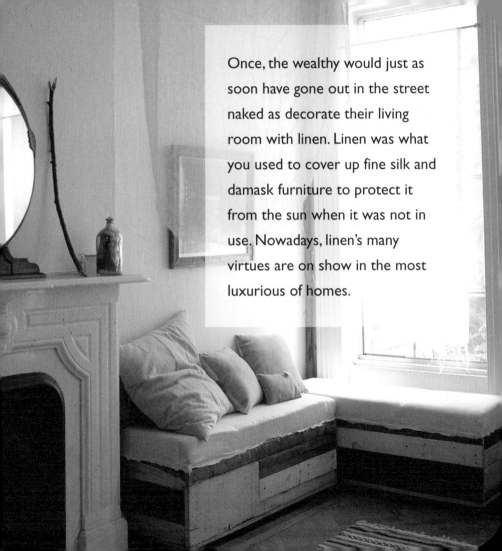

Once, the wealthy would just as soon have gone out in the street naked as decorate their living room with linen. Linen was what you used to cover up fine silk and damask furniture to protect it from the sun when it was not in use. Nowadays, linen's many virtues are on show in the most luxurious of homes.

Neutral colour schemes are perenially popular but there's always a danger that they can become bland or lacking in visual interest. Varying textures are the solution, and any room scheme will be enlivened by tactile linen, whether natural or dyed. For a decorative scheme that will delight the eye, add some leather, polished wood and woven cane into the mix.

# LAUNDERING LINEN

Linen is robust enough to withstand the toughest laundry treatments and the highest temperatures, so it's the perfect material for bedlinen, towels, napkins and tablecloths. By some miracle, every time it's washed, a subtle molecular change takes place around each fibre, so the fabric comes up looking just like new. Iron it while it's still damp, add spray starch if you choose, and you'll have fresh sheets and table linen that's fit for a prince.

IS NOT OLD WINE
WHOLESOMEST, OLD
PIPPINS TOOTHSOMEST,
OLD WOOD BURN
BRIGHTEST, OLD LINEN
WASH WHITEST? OLD
SOLDIERS, SWEETHEART,
ARE SUREST, AND OLD
LOVERS ARE SOUNDEST.

JOHN WEBSTER

# LAYING THE TABLE

To make a simple meal into a special occasion, just add linen. Nowadays, we do not have the time nor the inclination to embroider monograms or coat-of-arms on linen napkins, so why not cheat instead? Scour antiques markets or hunt out online specialists to track down antique table linens that will make instant heirlooms and that you'll be proud to display on the table. If you enjoy cooking, you could make your own jam and seal the pots in the traditional way with rounds of waxed paper, and cover with linen tied with a length of string. Serve up your homemade jam with a pot of tea, scones and cream on the side.

For centuries, households of note would have table linens and bed linens of the finest figured damask that would be handed down through the generations. Patterns included heraldic crests, mottoes, dates – even perhaps the name or initials of the person who commissioned the cloth. But damask was only for the wealthy. It was costly to produce and required an army of servants to keep it looking pristine.

# SLEEPING BEAUTY

Linen sheets are a far cry from easy-care cottons and non-iron synthetic polyesters. They require a lot of elbow work to iron them to a marble smoothness, but those who have slept between linen sheets swear that they would never sleep on anything else. There's something blissful and self-indulgent about the feel of linen next to the skin. The structure of the fibre makes it cool in summer, yet warm in winter. And you can choose from plain linens enlivened only by a contrasting stripe, or sheets edged in lace, ribbon, bows and tucks. Heavy white embroidery and delicate white lace inserts on white bedlinen are classics, reminiscent of the elaborate frosting on a wedding cake. For extra bedtime bliss and to help you sleep even more sweetly, scent your bedroom with lavender-filled linen pillows.

The bedroom is somewhere we need to feel secure, and bedroom textiles tend to say a lot about the concerns of a particular society. In some of the Greek islands, bed tents suspended from a hook in the ceiling and made of panels of embroidered linen announced to the world the power of the family that owned them. In the nineteenth century, many people were obsessed with cleanliness. Only crisp white linen sheets and austere iron bedsteads gave them the feeling that bedrooms were spotless and germ-free. The cool simplicity of this look will never go out of fashion, but now it appears soft and forgiving, a calm retreat from the hustle and bustle of busy modern life.

# WET AND WILD

Linen and water go well together.
The fabric is stronger when it's
wet, so is traditionally the fibre of
choice for ships' sails, fishermen's
nets and firemen's hoses. And it
looks good in the bathroom, too,
whether your taste is for the
faded grandeur of antique gilded
overmantel mirrors, old brass
taps and a rolltop tub, or the
sleek thrill of a minimal bathroom
kitted out in gleaming chrome
and polished stone.

You couldn't find a thirstier fabric than linen if you tried. For absorbency, nothing beats it, so the linen is often the choice for the finest face and guest towels. Many of these are made in a specially developed weave known as honeycomb weave or huckaback. The loose interlacing of the linen threads gives the finished fabric even greater absorbency. Many of the world's finest hotels offer linen bathtowels and robes and you can indulge in the same luxury at home.

# STONE

STONE IS THE FRAME
ON WHICH THE EARTH IS
MODELLED AND WHEREVER
IT CROPS OUT - THERE
THE ARCHITECT MAY
SIT AND LEARN

FRANK LLOYD WRIGHT

# SHELTER

From palaeolithic times to the twenty-first century, stone has provided us with both shelter and sanctuary. Ancient caves bear witness to the daily lives and preoccupations of our earliest ancestors. Later came tools and temples of stone that testified to the permanence of the gods, and stone-built fortifications and palaces to consolidate the power of rulers. We still marvel at the work of the ancient Greeks, Romans, Egyptians, Aztecs and Incas and wonder at the art of the Renaissance or the delicacy of the Taj Mahal. The beauty of stone is enduring.

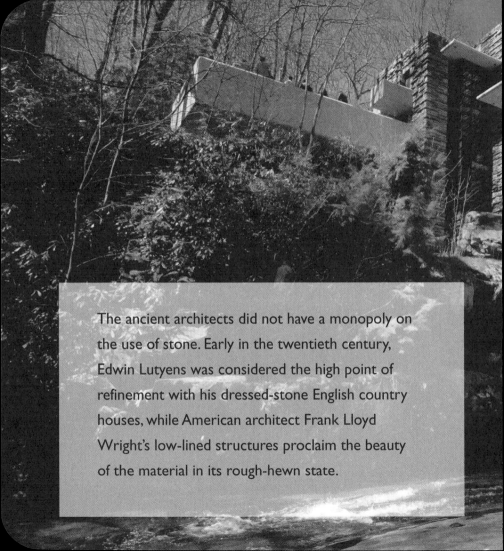

The ancient architects did not have a monopoly on the use of stone. Early in the twentieth century, Edwin Lutyens was considered the high point of refinement with his dressed-stone English country houses, while American architect Frank Lloyd Wright's low-lined structures proclaim the beauty of the material in its rough-hewn state.

Concrete was the darling of the Modern movement, but Le Corbusier, Breuer and Gropius all used stone too. And in more recent years, James Stirling and Quinlan Terry have chosen stone facings for a timeless classical look.

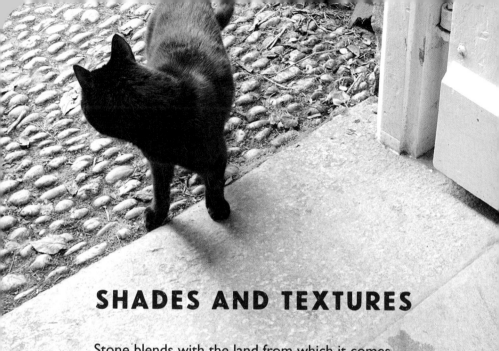

## SHADES AND TEXTURES

Stone blends with the land from which it comes —
a fact that did not escape the notice of even the
earliest architects. There are three general classes of
stone: igneous, sedimentary and metamorphic. Each
type is formed differently, hence their variations in
strength, colour, texture and composition.

Sandstones and limestones are sedimentary stones, formed by the compression of layers of sandy deposits, minerals and fossils in old sea and river beds. Their colours are generally tan, beige, cream and almost-white. Sandstone has a high silica content that gives it its sparkle, while in limestone you can often see remains of shells and fossils.

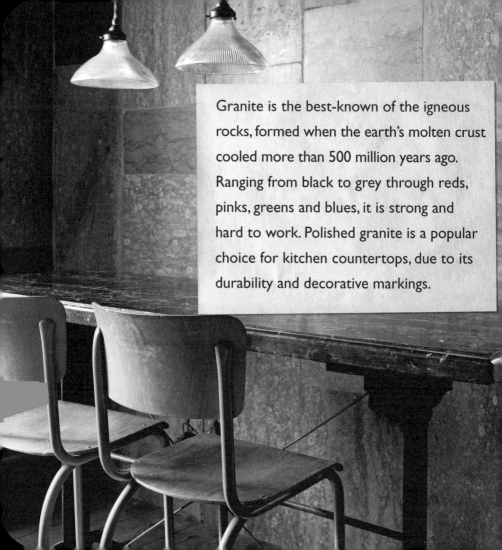

Granite is the best-known of the igneous rocks, formed when the earth's molten crust cooled more than 500 million years ago. Ranging from black to grey through reds, pinks, greens and blues, it is strong and hard to work. Polished granite is a popular choice for kitchen countertops, due to its durability and decorative markings.

Marble and slate are the metamorphic rocks – rocks changed through heat or pressure: marble from recrystallized limestone, slate from clay-rich rocks under pressure for millions of years. A softer stone with a crystalline glitter and waxy lustre, marble has been used for sculpture since ancient times and is considered one of the most luxurious and expensive of stones.

Stone's myriad shades and textures make it the perfect combination for numerous other natural materials. Always something of a luxury – in previous times, cost-cutting meant marble was often imitated by painting onto wood – happily, you need only use it sparingly. An exquisitely veined and polished marble countertop or an intricately carved antique mantelpiece bring understated elegance to any interior.

WRITE KINDNESS
IN MARBLE, AND
WRITE INJURIES
IN THE DUST

PERSIAN PROVERB

# LIVING SPACES

NOT SO VERY LONG AGO, WITH THE EXCEPTION OF FLAGSTONES AND COBBLES, STONE WAS THE PRESERVE OF THE WEALTHY. NOW, THANKS TO FAST, AFFORDABLE TRANSPORT, IT COMES FROM ALL OVER THE WORLD AND IS WITHIN THE REACH OF MANY.

As a material, stone is so versatile it can be used in any room of the house, but durability and easy maintenance make it a great choice for flooring in heavy-wear areas such as hallways and kitchens. And although it can be noisy and cold (try underfloor heating to combat these qualities) those minuses are far outweighed by its dramatic qualities and natural, elemental beauty.

Stone can look sleek and urban, or cosy and rustic. The trick lies in how it is cut and finished. Urban architects love gleaming right angles, while irregular, unpolished shapes speak of the country. Different types of stone suit different locations, but, as ever, it is fun to break the rules. Slate and pebbles are perfectly at home in the country, but try using them in a defiantly metropolitan apartment and enjoy the culture clash. Pebbles set in concrete bridge the divide between urban and rural, while split stones partner rough-hewn wood to perfection. And be the styling traditional or modern, in the kitchen slate and marble rule.

At home in bathrooms since the days of the Romans, stone is a must for sybaritic bathing. Choose a sink hewn from a single piece of stone or sit one atop a marble slab, but why stop there? Use granite for shelves. Clad the walls with marble. Lay limestone or slate over the floor. Fill your bath, lie back and indulge!

# ORNAMENT

We may not be able to replace our carpets with slate or laminate worksurfaces with granite, but it is possible to introduce stone into the home on a smaller scale – in the form of a bowl, a rough boulder or a collection of pebbles picked up on the beach. Such details are a means of bringing nature into a modern environment, where the emphasis is often on mass-produced machine-made objects. Stone makes reference to the natural world of which we are all a part.

IN THE NOT-SO-DISTANT PAST, WHEN STONE WAS USED AS ORNAMENT IN THE HOMES OF THE RICH, IT WAS IN THE FORM OF CLASSICAL DECORATIVE DETAILS SUCH AS PILLARS AND COLUMNS, MANTELPIECES AND MARBLE FLOORING. THE USE OF STONE PROCLAIMED WEALTH AND IMPORTANCE.

Nowadays, we can all enjoy stone in our homes. In contemporary design, it is often the details and how you place them that give pleasure and stone is perfect for this approach. Left to its own devices, a stone object can evoke the grandeur of a past age or the simplicity of a rustic kitchen. It can conjure up an image of a stroll along a mossy river bank or evoke the spirituality of the monumental standing stones that had such significance for our forefathers. Stone can decorate a table for simple outdoor eating or form part of a collection of found objects that create a tactile and intriguing display.

I SAW THE ANGEL IN THE
MARBLE AND CARVED
UNTIL I SET HIM FREE

MICHELANGELO BUONARROTI

# OUTSIDE

Stone started life out of doors,
formed many millennia ago by
movements of the earth's crust and
by intense heat and pressure deep
in its core, so it is no surprise that
it looks handsome in an outdoor
setting. Stone harmonizes with the
landscape to a degree that modern,
man-made materials, such as
concrete or glass, never will and it
weathers and grows old (or should
one say older?) beautifully, just like
fine antique furniture.

Decorating the garden with stone is not a new idea. The Romans did it, with marble statues, urns, columns and pools, while in the Renaissance, the art reached a peak. Today's look tends to be freer and less formal. Local stones pave a tranquil courtyard. A simple stone spout gushes into a broad stone basin. A pool of water lies peacefully in a stony surround. Or why not enjoy stone outside as nature intended – simply sitting on a windswept pebbly beach?

# WOOL

SHE SEEKETH
WOOL, AND FLAX,
AND WORKETH
WILLINGLY WITH
HER HANDS.

**PROVERBS 31:13**

# NATURAL

Wool can be gossamer fine, coarse and nubbly, and everything in between. Wear it, sleep beneath it, put it on your floors or use it to cover your furniture. Wherever it goes, wool is wonderful.

# SHEAR DELIGHT

Wool comes mainly from the fleece of domesticated sheep and has been used to make clothing and furnishings for as many as twenty-five thousand years. Prehistoric peoples clothed themselves in sheepskins and by about 3000 BC Sumerian men were depicted wearing what appear to be jaunty woven woollen skirts. The Bible tells of the white wool of Hebron that was traded in the markets of Damascus. And, since the Romans introduced sheep shearing, wool's quality and the range available to us has continued to improve.

During the middle ages, England was famed for its wool industry. Many magnificent churches and grand houses speak of the wealth of the wool merchants, who sold raw wool from English sheep to weavers in the Belgian cloth-making towns of Bruges and Ghent. To this day, the seat of the Lord Chancellor in the House of Lords is a large square cushion of wool named the 'Woolsack' – a permanent reminder of the historic importance of wool to the British economy.

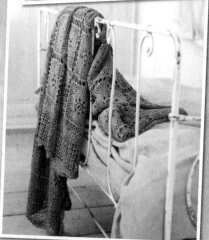

IN THESE WOULDS THERE FEED
IN GREAT NUMBERS, FLOCKES
OF SHEEPE LONG NECKED
AND SQUARE OF BULKE AND
BONE, BY REASON (AS IT IS
COMMONLY THOUGHT) OF THE
WEALLY AND HILLY SITUATION
OF THEIR PASTURAGE; WHOSE
WOOL BEING SO FINE AND
SOFT IS HAD IN PASSING
GREAT ACCOUNT AMONG
ALL NATIONS.

'BRITANNIA'
WILLIAM CAMDEN

Early settlers in North America had established a flock by 1609, but in the seventeenth century, the British government banned export of sheep to the Americas, or wool from it, in an attempt to combat any threat to the wool trade in the British Isles. Despite heavy punishments for wool trading in the colonies, the industry flourished and in 1662 a wool mill was built in Massachusetts.

Wool can be processed in two different ways. For the worsted method, uniform lengths of fairly fine fibres are used. These are combed and formed into strands for spinning into smooth fabrics. In the woollen system, fibres of mixed lengths are carded, then spun into a bulky, thick yarn. The finest wool is used for the finest of fabrics, while coarse wool often ends up as rugs, carpets and upholstery.

sheepskin-upholstered
Lamino lounge chair

hand-spun
undyed yarn

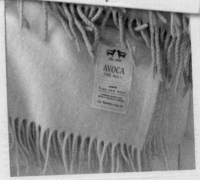

tweedy fringed throws

pure new wool blankets

WHETHER YOU OPT FOR
FLEECY SHEEPSKINS, A
FINELY WOVEN WOOL
SUIT, A TACTILE CASHMERE
JUMPER, A CHUNKY
HAND-KNITTED THROW OR
A VINTAGE WELSH BLANKET
THROWN OVER YOUR BED
OR THE BACK OF A SOFA,
WOOL WILL BRING YOU
CLOSER TO NATURE.

*tactile sheepskin softens a wooden chair*

*cosy felted wool blankets*

KNIT ONE, PURL ONE

People have been knitting for many centuries, but its origins are obscure. We do know, however, that by the seventeenth century, it had become a very popular pastime for ladies. And knitted fabrics have not lost any of their appeal in the years since. The Italian fashion company, Missoni, has made colourful, machine-made knits in fine yarns its trademark. But hand-knitting is for everyone.

It's satisfying, soothing and creative, and when you've finished, you've got something unique to wear. So pick up your needles and get going!

Wool's beautiful colours and textures serve as an antidote to the often harsh sensory effects of the modern world. Originally wool was dyed using natural plant and animal dyes – woad resulted in soft blues; lichens in mauves; and a certain mollusc gave the famous Tyrian purple of antiquity. Alexander the Great's father was buried in woollen clothes dyed this colour. Wool dyes very well. The dye bonds right inside the fibre. And modern dyes resist fading too.

Wool from sheep is only one of many possibilities. There are featherlight yet surprisingly cosy wools that are produced from the fleeces or fur of other animals. Alpaca and vicuña come from animals related to the llama; cashmere and pashm are the soft, luxurious wools of animals from Kashmir and Tibet; and angora is the long hair of Angora goats or rabbits. These are all luxury fabrics – rarer and less hard-wearing than sheep's wool.

I EARN THAT I EAT, GET THAT
I WEAR, OWE NO MAN HATE,
ENVY NO MAN'S HAPPINESS,
GLAD OF OTHER MEN'S
GOOD, CONTENT WITH MY
HARM, AND THE GREATEST
OF MY PRIDE IS TO
SEE MY EWES GRAZE AND
MY LAMBS SUCK.

'AS YOU LIKE IT'
WILLIAM SHAKESPEARE

# COVER UP

Wool is the ultimate when it comes to comfort. Unlike synthetics, which can absorb only about two per cent of their own weight in moisture before they start to feel damp and clammy, wool can cope with as much as thirty per cent. And because it disperses water from the skin, wool also helps keep your temperature steady. Wool also gently moulds to your body, then springs back into shape, making it comfortable as well as practical.

Bedouin tribesmen wrap themselves in flowing wool robes woven from camel hair for comfort in a harsh climate that can scorch by day and freeze at night. Goat or camel hair was also woven to create their tents.

Navajo Indians wrapped themselves in brightly coloured blankets with bold geometric patterns, while the Coast Salish peoples of the Pacific Northwest wove their beautiful twill blankets from the hair of their tame white dogs. A modern handwoven blanket, edged in blanket stitch, is a classic too.

Wool was once a basic necessity of life – among the fabrics that early American settlers imported from the mother country was the aptly named sturdy woollen cloth named 'fearnought'.

Nowadays in the modern developed world, wool may not be an essential but it offers us a sense of psychological comfort nonetheless. Mohair blankets, fluffy sheepskins and sumptuous pashminas strewn across the bed not only look stylish and keep you warm, they make you feel good too. Wool is conducive to deeper, longer sleep, too. Studies suggest that wool bedding – duvets, pillows and mattress toppers – can improve how people sleep, particular if they suffer from skin conditions such as eczema. How comforting!

# WOOLLY WARMERS

Wool of every type is the cosiest fabric to wrap yourself up in on a chilly winter's day. A soft, fluffy sheepskin jacket, cashmere socks, a pair of handknitted Fair Isle gloves or a herringbone-weave tweed scarf will keep out even the most biting of winds.

Felt is a variation on wool knits that boasts superb insulating properties. It is a non-woven textile made by matting, condensing and pressing wool (or other natural materials) so that the fibres interlock to create a strong, durable fabric that can be cut without fraying.

Felt isn't just warm and wind-proof, it also keeps out the wet. Originating in Central Asia, since ancient times, the nomadic tribesman of this region have used felt to make clothing, saddle covers, blankets and slippers as well as for their traditional tents, or yurts. Felting for art has enjoyed a renaissance in recent years and many contemporary textile artists are exploring the possibilities of the medium.

Woollen rugs will bring bring warmth and comfort to any home. In period homes, antique Oriental woollen rugs on polished parquet floors add a traditional touch of warmth. For a fresh yet cosy interior, look to Scandinavia. Clean lines, natural textures and monochrome colour schemes typify modern Scandi style. Warm things up with plump feather pillows, sheepskins strewn across the floor and a wealth of wool blankets in moody colours, and you have a contemporay look that is snug and welcoming yet stylish.

# FASHION STATEMENT

Warmth is something we feel on a psychological level as much as we do a physical one, and what better way to achieve that sense of wellbeing than to surround yourself with nature's handiwork? Man-made materials and neon hues have their place, but for a sense of warmth, comfort and security, we need to go back to our roots. For urban rustics, an interior sporting sheepskin rugs, furniture upholstered in soft, forgiving wool and cosy crocheted throws will create a homespun vibe that makes a house a home.

Wool and interiors are a match made in heaven. Wool shrugs off dirt; it is strong, resilient and looks good for years, making it the perfect fabric for practical rugs and inviting sofas. The latest wool fabrics for the home come in so many guises that you're bound to find one that seizes your imagination. There are nubbly twisted and tufted carpets for floors and tactile upholstery fabrics as well as light-as-down cobwebby knits and fluffy, cosy sheepskins. Non-woven wools, such as felts, can bring a homespun, crafty effect, while special-effect yarns shot through with sparkling metallics add a note of glamour. Whether your tastes tend towards the modern or the traditional, wool is truly versatile.

# PICTURE CREDITS

1 ph Catherine Gratwicke/The family home of Gina Portman of Folk at Home www.folkathome.com 2 ph Hans Blomquist 7 ph Paul Massey/ Naja Lauf 8–9 ph Catherine Gratwicke/Oliver Heath and Katie Weiner – sustainable architecture, interior and jewellery design 10 al & br ph Catherine Gratwicke/The cabin of Hanne Borge and her family in Norway 10 ar ph Earl Carter/The home of Rick Livingston and Jim Brawders at Quogue, New York on Long Island 10 bl ph Debi Treloar/www.aureliemathigot.com, 12 ph Paul Ryan/Summer house at Hvasser, of Astir Eidsbo and Tore Lindholm 13 ph Paul Ryan/ A house designed by Ilkka Suppanen in Finland 14–15 ph Catherine Gratwicke/The cabin of Hanne Borge and her family in Norway 16 ph Paul Ryan/Ritva Puotila's summerhome in Finland 17 ph Earl Carter/The family home of Hanne Dalsgaard and Henrik Jeppesen in Zealand, Denmark 19 ph Debi Treloar/The family home of designers Ulla Koskinen and Sameli Rantanen in Finland 21 ph Catherine Gratwicke/The family home of the interior designer Larissà van Seumeren in the Netherlands 22 ph Anna Williams

23 ph Catherine Gratwicke/The cabin of Hanne Borge and her family in Norway 24 ph Debi Treloar/La villa des Ombelles, the family home of Jean-Marc Dimanche Chairman of V.I.T.R.I.O.L. agency www.vitriol-factory.com 25 ph Catherine Gratwicke/www.stylexclusief.nl 27 ph Earl Carter/The home of Cary Tamarkin and Mindy Goldberg on Shelter Island 28 ph Paul Ryan/The summerhome of Elina Helenius and Mika Mahlberg in Finland 29 ph Paul Ryan/Aki Wahlman's summerhome in Finland 30 ph Paul Ryan/The summerhouse of Peter Morgan at the Bjäte peninsula (in the north-west of Scania) 31 ph Paul Ryan/Summer house at Hvasser, of Astir Eidsbo and Tore Lindholm 32 ph Claire Richardson/Stéphane Olivier's home in Paris 33 ph Polly Wreford/ The family home of Fiona and Alex Cox of www.coxandcox.co.uk 34 l and 35 al ph Jan Baldwin/Kristin Krogstad Interior Architect, www.thedrawingroom.no 34 c ph Polly Wreford/The home of stylist Twig Hutchinson in London 34 r ph Debi Treloar/Mariella Ienna textile designer, Via Tomaso Lo Cascio 16; Palermo 90142 ; Sicily; mariella.ienna.design @gmail.com 35 bl ph Catherine Gratwicke/Oliver Heath and Katie Weiner – sustainable architecture, interior and jewellery design 35 ar ph Earl Carter/The home of Rick Livingston

and Jim Brawders at Quogue, New York on Long Island 36 ph Debi Treloar 38 ph Anna Williams/The home of Jocie Sinauer, owner of Red Chair, on Warren in Hudson, New York 39 ph Polly Wreford/The home in Lewes of Justin and Heidi Francis, owner of Flint www.flintcollection.com 40–41 ph Catherine Gratwicke/The home of Jonathan Sela and Megan Schoenbachler 43 ph Catherine Gratwicke/The cabin of Hanne Borge and her family in Norway 44–45 ph Debi Treloar/House in Vaud, Switzerland designed by Maria Speake and Adam Hills of Retrouvius 46 ph Catherine Gratwicke/Oliver Heath and Katie Weiner – sustainable architecture, interior and jewellery design 47 ph Debi Treloar 48 ph Catherine Gratwicke/The home of Erica Farjo and David Slade 49 ph Rachel Whiting/Victoria Smith, editor sfgirlbybay.com 50 ph Debi Treloar/The house of stylist Reini Smit in the Netherlands, reini@quicknet.nl 51 al ph Catherine Gratwicke/Oliver Heath and Katie Weiner – sustainable architecture, interior and jewellery design 51 ar ph Polly Wreford/ London house by Sarah Delaney Design 51 b ph Debi Treloar/The home of Jacques Bastide in Arles, France 52 ph Debi Treloar/La villa des Ombelles, the family home of Jean-Marc Dimanche Chairman of V.I.T.R.I.O.L. agency www.vitriol-factory.com 53 ph Debi Treloar/The home of antiques dealer and interior designer Oliver Gustav in Copenhagen 55 ph Earl Carter/The family

home of Hanne Dalsgaard and Henrik Jeppesen in Zealand, Denmark 56 ph Chris Tubbs/Vermont Shack/Ross Anderson, anderson architects 57 ph Pia Tryde 59 ph Earl Carter/The summerhouse of Helene Blanche and Jannik Martensen-Larsen, owner of Tapet Café in Copenhagen www.tapet-café.com 60 ph Debi Treloar/The home of Jacques Bastide in Arles, France 62 © Bastiaan Wesseling/Alamy 63 ph Debi Treloar/ Hans Blomquist's home in Paris (www.agentbauer.com) 64 and 65 a ph Lisa Cohen/Anna McDougall's London home 65 b ph Lisa Cohen/ The home of Lars Wiberg of Pour Quoi in Copenhagen 67 ph Hans Blomquist 68 ph Debi Treloar/The home of Nadia Yaron and Myriah Scruggs of Nightwood in Brooklyn 69 Merlyn Severn/ Picture Post/Getty Images 70 ph Claire Richardson/ Josephine Ryan Antiques, 63 Abbeville Road, London SW4 9JW 71 ph Lucinda Symons 72 ph Debi Treloar/Hans Blomquist's home in Paris (www.agentbauer.com) 73 ph Claire Richardson/ The home of Leida Nassir-Pour of Warp & Weft in Hastings 74 ph Lisa Cohen/Cloth House, 47 Berwick Street, London W1F 8SJ. www.clothhouse.com 75 ph Debi Treloar/Vox Populi, the studio of the artist/designer Pascale Palun, in Avignon. 76–77 ph Debi Treloar/Stella Willing stylist/designer and owner of this house in Amsterdam 78 ph Hans Blomquist 79 ph Debi Treloar/The home of antiques dealer and interior designer Oliver Gustav in Copenhagen **80** ph Lisa Cohen/Anna Mcdougall's London Home. **81** ph Jan Baldwin/The home of Sophie Lambert, owner of Au Temps des Cerises in France **82** al ph Debi Treloar/The home of Nadia Yaron and Myriah Scruggs of Nightwood in Brooklyn **82** ar and bl ph Lisa Cohen/The designer Clare Teed's home in Hampton, www.sashawaddell.com **82** br ph Debi Treloar **83** a ph Debi Treloar/The home of Kristin Norris and Trevor Lunn, Philadelphia **83** b ph Peter Cassidy **84** ph Debi Treloar/Josephine Ryan **85** ph Lisa Cohen/The designer Nina Hartmann's home in Sweden, www.vintagebynina.com **86** ph Claire Richardson/www.les-sardines.com **87** ph Debi Treloar/The home of Nadia Yaron and Myriah Scruggs of Nightwood in Brooklyn **88** ph Hans Blomquist **90** ph Polly Wreford/The home of family Voors in the Netherlands designed by Karin Draaijer **91** ph Hans Blomquist **93** ph Debi Treloar/The Home of Mark and Sally Bailey www.baileyshome.com **95** l ph Steve Painter **95** r ph Carolyn Barber **96** ph Claire Richardson/The home of Jean-Louis Fages and Matthieu Ober in Nimes **97** ph Polly Wreford/London home of Michael Bains and Catherine Woram **99** ph Debi Treloar/The home of artist and antiques dealer and interior designer Monique Meij-Beekman in the Netherlands **100** ph Debi Treloar/ The family home of Harriet Maxwell Macdonald of Ochre.net in New York **101** ph Hans Blomquist **102** ph Earl Carter/ Robert Young, Robert Young Architecture & Interiors www.ryarch.com **104–105** ph Debi Treloar/Josephine Ryan **106** ph Rachel Whiting/The home of Maria Carr of www.dreamywhitesonline.com **107** ph Debi Treloar/The home of Nadia Yaron and Myriah Scruggs of Nightwood in Brooklyn **108** ph Paul Massey/The Barton's seaside home in West Sussex: www.thedodo.co.uk **109** ph Debi Treloar/The home of Nadia Yaron and Myriah Scruggs of Nightwood in Brooklyn **110** ph Paul Massey/ Hôtel Le Sénéchal, Ars en Ré, designed by Christophe Ducharme Architecte **112** DeAgostini/Getty Images **114–115** ph Debi Treloar **116–117** Spiegl/ ullstein bild via Getty Images **118** ph Jan Baldwin/The home of textile designer Richard Smith and art dealer Andrew Blackman **119** l ph Jan Baldwin/The family home of Ursula and Toby Falconer **119** r ph Debi Treloar/Velasco Vitali (velascovitali@gmail.com) and architect Arturo (arturo.montanelli@gmail.com) **120** ph Jan Baldwin/Botelet Farm, A special place to stay in Cornwall www.botelet.com **121** ph Simon Brown **122** ph Paul Massey **123** l ph Debi Treloar/The home of James and Maria Backhouse in London, designed by Maria Speake and Adam Hills of Retrouvius **123** r ph Claire Richardson **124–125** ph Andrew Wood/ Isosceles Land Pte Ltd's house in Singapore designed by Chan Soo Khian of SCDA Architects **126** ph Debi Treloar/The

163 ph Debi Treloar/The home of the artist Claudy Jongstra in the Netherlands 164–165 Nadeem Khawar/Getty Images 166 ph Catherine Gratwicke/The cabin of Hanne Borge and her family in Norway 167 a ph Debi Treloar/The house of stylist Reini Smit in the Netherlands, reini@quicknet.nl 167 b ph Polly Wreford/Foster Cabin designed by Dave Coote (www.beachstudios.co.uk) 169 ph Anna Williams/39 Bea B&B owned by Bea Mombaers in Knokke-Le Zoute, Belgium (www.bea-bb.com) 170–171 Adrian Streun/ASAblanca via Getty Images 172 Michael Hall/Getty Images 173 ph Polly Wreford/Abigail Ahern's home in London 174 al ph Paul Ryan/The summerhouse of Peter Morgan at the Bjäte peninsula (in the north-west of Scania) 174 ar ph Debi Treloar/The home of the artist Claudy Jongstra in the Netherlands 174 bl ph Polly Wreford/A London house by Sarah Delaney Design 174 br ph James Fennell/Amanda Pratt, Creative Director, Avoca 175 a ph Anna Williams/The home of the designer Josephine Ekström, owner of Lily and Oscar, in Sweden 175 b ph Paul Massey/The home in Denmark of Charlotte Lynggaard, designer of Ole Lynggaard Copenhagen 176–178 ph Claire Richardson 179 ph Emma Mitchell and Becky Maynes 180–181 ph Debi Treloar/La villa des Ombelles, the family home of Jean-Marc Dimanche Chairman of V.I.T.R.I.O.L. agency www.vitriol-factory.com 183 ph Claire Richardson 184 ph Polly Wreford/Siobhán McKeating's home in London 185 ph Alex Adams/Design Pics/Getty Images 185 r ph Philippe Henry/Getty Images 186 ph Catherine Gratwicke/The family home of Gina Portman of Folk at Home www.folkathome.com 187 ph Andrew Wood/Mary Shaw's Sequana apartment in Paris 188 ph Polly Wreford/The family home of the stylist Anja Koops and chef Alain Parry in Amsterdam 191 Transcendental Graphics/Getty Images 192 ph Catherine Gratwicke/The cabin of Hanne Borge and her family in Norway 193 ph Polly Wreford 194 ph Penny Wincer 195–196 ph Debi Treloar/The home of the artist Claudy Jongstra in the Netherlands 198 a ph Jan Baldwin/The London home of William Palin of SAVE Britain's Heritage 198 b ph Debi Treloar/The home of artist and antiques dealer and interior designer Monique Meij-Beekman in the Netherlands 199 ph Claire Richardson/The B&B Camellas-Lloret, designed and owned by Annie Moore near Carcassonne 200 ph Catherine Gratwicke/Oliver Heath and Katie Weiner – sustainable architecture, interior and jewellery design 203 ph Rachel Whiting/Niki Brantmark of My Scandinavian Home (myscandinavianhome.blogspot.com).